POEMS

Daniel Engelke Jr.

Copyright © 2023 Daniel Engelke Jr.
All rights reserved
First Edition

Fulton Books
Meadville, PA

Published by Fulton Books 2023

ISBN 979-8-88982-327-8 (paperback)
ISBN 979-8-88982-328-5 (digital)

Printed in the United States of America

Gone but not forgotten. To those people and
relatives who did not know I have this talent and
the opportunity to put into a published book.

Thinking of Her

Our song is playing on the radio.
The warmth of the sun reminds me of your smile.
Whenever I look at the stars in the night sky, they
remind me of her eyes.
My ears hear your name being mentioned by someone
else.
Whenever I reach out my hand around you are not
near me.
When I'm home alone, I just want you to be by my
side.
My dreams have you as an angel by my side.
Your picture is a faded memory whenever I see it.
I always believed we could always be together as a
couple forever in the years ahead.

Written by D. A. Engelke Jr.

Somewhere I Will Find Her

Every night I feel so lonely without her.
There are people who don't think I
will never find this woman.
Without a smile on my face shows up as a
frown and tells a tale of frustration.
I still believe there is a woman in this
world who can make me happy.
Here in my heart there is a dream that is not broken.
Establishing a friendship will always
be the first priority for me.
I will be looking north and south, east or west for her.
What can I say to you?
When I am so in love with this woman.
If I don't find her the earth will be the
loneliest place to live for this man.

The Very Thought of Her

Days can pass by before I could see her again.
A smile greets me whenever she enters the room.
My heart beats faster, faster, faster, and even faster.
The smell of perfume in the air tells me she is nearby.
Whenever I hear our song, I can either
sing it or have tears in my eyes.
Is able to calm me down whenever
my anger flares up.
When she gives you an expected
birthday card a day after the event.
Our friendship will continue to grow every time we
can keep each the company on a lonely evening.
Hearing her voice tells me she is around
to listen to what's on my mind.
Giving gifts like a holiday cards to show I
truly respect the woman in herself.
I would never put down her in front of anybody.
Never looking away without a tear in her eye.
If there is time to be spent together it will not
be measured by a watch nor by the moments.
Intelligence is one of the qualities
I look for in a woman.
I can tell her these three little words, "I love you."
The hardest part could be saying
"goodbye" every time she walks away.

Whenever I See Her Again?

The clock keeps ticking the seconds, minutes, and
hours.
Even the days, weeks, and months are washing away
like the ocean's tide.
Phone calls can never replace catching sight of her in
person.
How can I say "I missed you in my life" to her?
There are a lot of lonely days and lonely nights for me.
I ask the question How can she mend my broken
heart?
What will it take to get her back into this guy's life?
She had a role in my life at one time.
I didn't want to lose our relationship between this
man and you.
I want you to fill the void in my life.
Our time together will not be measured by our watches
but by the moments.
When will I see her again?

Does She Love Me?

Her smile heals this man's broken heart.
There's a man in me who respects
a woman's private life.
Days can pass by without seeing her.
Laughter fills the air whenever we
are together as a couple.
Only time can heal the wound of our love.
Even the nights can be lonely for me.
We are a couple that can endure the test of time.
Whenever I hear our favorite love song it will
tell me all roads lead in the right direction.
Do you believe a love could run so strong?
All around us people fall in love and get married.
Every day I see you I call it lucky!
If heaven is missing an angel, then I
must have an angel by my side.

Where Are My Friends?

We are separated by many miles and a long winding
road.
I looked to the north and to the south.
I try to contact them by telephone calls or writing
letters.
Seasons come and go like night and day.
Each one is mature and aged like a good bottle of wine.
Our friendship comes and goes like an ocean tide on
the tide on the beach.
Departing from my life is just a normal part of grow-
ing into an adult.
I take another look this time to the east and to the
west.
With a little help from all of you I have become a
leader.
We together as a group can make a contribution to
our great country.

Searching for Ms. Right

When I look for your smile, it will warm my heart and
soul.
The day you departed my life I had a tear in my eye.
Our friendship can endure a lot of emotions for the
good and bad moments.
Seasons come and go like the sands of time.
Our time together will not be measured by any watch
but by moments.
I look toward the north and to the south with no trace
of her nowhere to be found.
The night light reaches out to show you the tender-
ness I had for you whenever we were together on
a date.
And some days I feel so alone.
The long winding road is still long.
I made a final look first at the east and next to the west
for a final look.
She could have a key to this guy's heart.
How can I stop this hurting in my heart?

Relationships

Some of our relationships blossom like flowers in the
spring and others don't.
Others can go out like the tide hits the beach.
Some friends can make them last a lifetime.
Before we know it, they can erode before our eyes.
Loved ones cherish their relationships over the years.
There are truly once-in-a-lifetime ones that come in
and out like night and day.
We hold a lot of different relationships with all rela-
tives in our families.
The tougher ones are the people who love you the
most and die unexpectedly.

The Essential Character of a Friend

Their own self-discipline will always
be shown among other people.
There is always a sense of friendship
over time you see them.
Compassion comes through whenever
they find their true love in life.
Courage goes on with life and its
many challenges day by day.
Always showing their honesty among
their other friends and family.
With all their hard work could pay off for
a better future in the years ahead.
A faith to succeed in long-range goals in their lives.
With perseverance, they will be able to get
through days, weeks, months, and even years.
Loyalty comes with the friendships for
each one you want to last a lifetime.

Will She Come Back?

The years have eroded like an ocean's beach.
Going our separate ways didn't mean an end of a
    friendship to me.
The highlights in your hair remind me of a rainbow.
The seasons come and go without you by my side.
Every mile I travel I am always thinking about her.
Her smile warmed my heart as the sun shines during
    the day.
I looked to the north first and next to the south.
Whenever I have thoughts of your departure, I put my
    head down.
I don't want her to fade away from my life.
Being all alone for the rest of my life was not part of
    the plan.
I made two final looks, first to the east and the last to
    the west.
I ask myself this question, "Will she come back?"

When We Were Together

In her presence, I am a perfect gentleman.
Our hugs and kisses are given out
at the tender moments.
We can both put our worries away for the day.
The days and nights seem to last forever.
The mood and setting are both to our likeness.
I can say to her "I am glad you're
the woman in my life."
Every beat of our hearts goes along with
the music we enjoy listening to.
People can take notice of how both of us are
two special people in each other's lives.
The atmosphere we create is all our own.
We can express our love ninety percent of each day.

Finding Happiness
in My Life

Lonely days.
Empty nights.
The sun comes out and I don't
have a woman by my side.
I look for an angel from north to the
south as well as to the east and west.
Some days I feel all alone with nobody around.
There are roadblocks for women who
have relationships with other guys.
The tears I shed tell people there has
been sadness and tragedy in my life.
I've been searching for so long for a woman.
Seasons come and go I look for the rainbow
in which I might find that special lady.
I never thought I would be alone.

My Lonely Heart

There are a lot of tears every day.
I don't sleep well at night thinking about it.
I hit roadblocks like boyfriends, fiancés, or husbands
Each day gets to be a long winding road that has no
     end.
Searching goes on consistently every waking hour.
Dreams at night turn out to be nightmares.
There is no sunshine when she is not around.
I know there has been heartache and pain.
The tears I cry are out of fear I feel all by myself.
How can you mend my broken heart?

A Day with Her by My Side

I realize she puts my mind at ease.
The sunlight glows off her like an angel in heaven.
I don't want to see the tears in our eyes
when we leave each other arms.
Holding hands tells us, we are still
in love with each other.
I want her sense of humor to always
put a smile on my face.
I will always lose myself in the blues of her eyes.
Life is too short for both of us to end
our relationship right now.
She is the love of my life and I don't want to deny it
The pressures inside my head are at
ease when I am around her.
We can recall memories when we
are alone with each other.
Let us set the mood by playing our
favorite music on a stereo.
I can say these four words to her every time
whenever we are alone: "I love you, darling."

These Are My Friends

Each one lives either north or south,
east or west in these United States.
Recalling memories brings them
together to hear stories of the past
The years have not changed our
friendship over this period of time.
Our world has changed its outlook just
like them when they were younger,
They are unique in their own ways of life.
Single, marriage does not change anything in
the period of time we have been friends.
It's not one day or week that I think about them.
Not being around my friends is the
hardest hit my heart takes every day.
Whenever you hear our laughter, it shows how
much fun we enjoy each other's company.
Our time together was not measured
by a watch but by moments.
Saying goodbye is the hardest part when
we depart to go our separate ways.
"These are my friends, and no one
can take them out of my life!"

There Is Something Special about Her

Possess two eyes that shine like
the stars on a clear night.
Does not want to give up on our friendship
but strengthens it every day.
A smile that tells me I am here to support you.
Hearing this woman's voice inspires me to
continue on every day with my life.
Always polite with those special gifts given to her.
Well-mannered around people who
enjoy this woman's company.
These would be sad empty faces from
both of us if were to break up.
I can always embrace this gal at times when
we're happy to see each other or say goodbye.
A photograph on the wall will remind
me how special she really is to me.
There will always be a special place in my
heart and soul for this angel in my life.

I Believe in Her

Trusting the secrets we share with each other.
In a friendship that continues on every day.
Seeing a smile that tells me she likes to be by my side.
I can always express my feelings toward this
woman in a greeting card and even in a poem.
We are two mature adults on this good earth.
Her lifestyle has been adjusting to a
modern twenty-first-century living.
I always got her in my mind every day of the week.
Staying in touch is one way we both can count
on being a caring person in each other's life.
Being alone, I can only hope everything is alright.
I am believing in her, showing we
trust each other's private lives.

She's My Friend

We can talk about our troubles with each other.
She makes sure in public maturity is shown
among her friends and family including myself
Her style is a continuing thing
during her everyday life.
Expressing feelings come out whenever
she wants them to be shown.
Whenever I am around this woman, I want
to be putting on my best smile for her.
Showing her caring side always gets my attention.
I will want you by my side whenever I
have truly good moments in my life.
Maturity has made her a better person over the years.
Her sense of humor always gets me to
laugh on the really bad days of my life.
Season's come and season's go like
our ages as we grow older.
Reflecting on our memories is something
that nobody can take away from us.
Thanks for being my friend over the years.

You're My Best Friend

When you make a phone call to me when I feel sad.
I can send a greeting card to put a smile on her face.
We can exchange messages on social media to stay in
    touch.
Our song can always tell me I am thinking of you.
Wishing you were here whenever there is a special
    event occurs.
"Seasons come and go" means I miss her every day.
Memories can be reflected along with laughter; when
    we relive them together.
Photographs show me a moment in time we shared
    together.
In times of sadness, she can comfort me in her own
    way.
Caring for each other is one thing we share in this spe-
    cial friendship of ours.
I will always want to say good things about her when I
    am around her.
When you are not beside me means I still have you
    inside my heart.
Defending our friendship when there are disbelievers
    get in the way.
It's the angel in you that brings out the man in me.
I can't leave her alone without me in her life.
The sun is always shining down on us whenever we
    get together.

There is always a piece of heaven in her heart and a
halo above her head.
Even though you are so far away, you will always be in
my mind.
Nothing could be good as a best friend who can care
about me when I need her at the right time.
Phone calls always bring the closing words "I miss
you."
Between us, our friendship will go on, on, on, and on.

My Friends

They are supportive and on my side like teammates.
Each one listens and gossips during the day.
I have gained a lot of them either through high school,
     work, relationships, and pen pals.
I keep in contact either in person, by letters, by phone
     calls, and even by cards in the mail.
The ones I had in my life for a short time I wished they
     stayed around longer.
Their ages don't hurt our friendship, but it helps
     strengthens it for the years ahead.
I can see each one of them is truly mature in public.
They are professionals in today's business world.
Some of these people I grew up with are still a part of
     my life.
Some of them play small roles and others play larger
     roles in this guy's life.
Each one cherishes life in their own ways.
Their private lives are hardly discussed on the job and
     in their spare time.
Favors always seem to pay off like rewards in life.
Sometimes they come to see me unexpectedly.
It's hard to keep every one of them to stay in my life.
To all of my friends past and present thanks for all the
     memories you have given me over the years.

What Is Friendship?

Friendships flow deeper than an ocean.
Caring for each other runs longer than a river.
Recalling the memories brings
laughter and sometimes tears.
Between friends there are good
moments even bad moments.
Helping each other builds an everlasting friendship.
Respect goes with any friendship.
Friends listen to each other's problems
and offer advice to them.
Friendships always last a lifetime.

Without You

I have tears in my eyes.
My ears don't hear your name anymore.
My nose can't smell your perfume.
I can't put a smile on my face.
My footsteps get lost in the sand.
My voice is not speaking your name to you anymore.
There is no more sunshine in my life.
I lose my sense of direction.
There is no love in my heart.
The earth will be the loneliest place to live.

My Woman

She's a loving, mother, wife, and lifelong friend.
Her smile warms my heart and soul like oatmeal.
I comfort her in times of sorrow and grief.
I tend to her whenever she might be sick.
We celebrate our special occasions during the calen-
    dar year.
The sunlight shows off her beauty each time it shines
    down on her.
Buying flowers tells her how much I love her role in
    my life.
I always give her a comfortable hug for support.
Her baking and cooking skills are just like my mother's.
Being mature put this man's mind at ease.
She values her quality of life every day.
I know without her I would be lonely day and at night.
Every day, I say to myself how lucky I am to have her
    as my woman.
My woman, she is truly an angel in this guy's life.

Where Is She?

The sun is coming out, and I didn't see the light.
I almost thought it was the start of night.
Seasons come and seasons go.
I looked to the north, the south, the east, and the west.
The sunlight does not cast your shadow on the ground.
Remembering your smile gets harder with each pass-
	ing day.
You saw a tear in my eye and just walked away.
My hand keeps reaching out for you whenever I call
	for you.
Memories of you are being washed away as the tide
	comes in and out from the ocean.
The miles cannot be replaced by anything, but you.
Our friendship has endured the years either with hap-
	piness or sadness.
The days keep getting longer and longer with each
	passing second.
My memory has flashbacks not photographs of you.
Being apart from you hurts this man's lonely heart.
Whenever I see your picture, I can't even put a smile
	on my face.
I really cannot believe you are out of my life.

Friends

Who are they?
Helping them out is part of the unwritten
oath in "What Is Friendship?" pledge.
Some move to a new area in order to
begin a new life for themselves.
There are lifetime friends between husbands
and wives plus brothers and sisters.
Happy moments are always celebrated
among the closest of friends.
Each one has a different lifestyle
in each of their homes.
Years change everyone's relationships
between the sexes.
They help us celebrate good times and
comfort us in times of sorrow.
Their relationships dry up like an arid desert
Keeping in contact with them shows a caring heart
They are separated by miles and direction
either by north, south, east, or west
To all my friends past and present thanks
for supporting me over the years.

About the Author

Daniel was born in Duluth, Minnesota. He and his parents later moved to Saginaw, Michigan, where he graduated from Douglas MacArthur High School. He had his first poem printed in the high school newspaper. His real success came when he submitted a poem for a contest in 1998, which awarded him a spot in their book. He started on more poetry and released a few more for other collections. He even did one in from his classmates. He moved to Bay City, Michigan, to continue his poetry writing. He resides and works for the local Walmart superstore. He is an active member of the Loyal of Moose in Saginaw. At his lodge, he served as a board member for four years. He would like to thank his family and friends for their support over the years. This is his first book of poetry.